Me, Myself, and Ivana

Ivana Korovesovska

Creation Publishing Group
www.creationpublishing.com

© 2013 by Ivana Korovesovska
Published by Creation Publishing Group LLC
1219 Nikki Lane, Stafford, Texas 77477
www.creationpublishing.com

ISBN: 978-0-9641894-1-6

Printed in the United States of America

All rights reserved. No part of this book may be reproduced, stored in a retrieval system or transmitted in any form or by any means without the prior written permission of the publishers, except by a reviewer who may quote brief passages in a review to be printed in a newspaper, magazine or journal.

Library of Congress Control Number: 2013946916

ACKNOWLEDGMENTS

It's funny how you never really liked the ocean and you were born a swimmer.

It's inevitable to note that my common cynicism in collision with a huge amount of pure affection I felt over the past 29 years of my life, takes most of the "blame" for the following pages. The process of transforming a rock garden into a field of roses makes me reconsider my entire existence. I find a single drop of hope each time I smell the thorns of life looking at that never ending beauty, worthy of the effort we put in everyday living. Sometimes we forget that even the most perfect things in life have sweetest little flaws, making them even more beautiful…

I dedicate this small collection of poems to my family, my closest friends (reducing over the years), the lost but never forgotten one and only that changed my life, but mostly I'd like to thank Michael first of all for: believing in me, supporting me and giving me this opportunity I never thought I'd get. I guess he is a great reminder that some dreams do come true ☺

In order to submit to the truth, I give you a piece of my mind and soul…Enjoy ☺

FOREWORD

The intention of poetry is to give you a glimpse inside the mind and heart of a writer. When the words touch our hearts, and cause us to think, then the writer has achieved their goal.

In her beautifully written book of poetry, Ivana Korovesovska invites us to come into her world as she shares her heart and soul with thought provoking eloquence and warmth. Like a master painter, she paints a picture of beauty and depth with her words that captures our hearts and warms our souls.

Join Ivana as she takes you on a journey of contemplation and discovery that allows you to see who she really is and what goes on inside the mind and heart of a true artist and writer.

Coach Michael Taylor

TABLE OF CONTENTS

6 AM	15
GOLDEN MOUNTAINTOP	16
HANG ON	17
HOLD STILL	18
LIGHT IN THE DARK	19
WALKING DEAD	20
VOLCANIC DREAMS	21
SIP OF THE HEART	22
THE APPLE TREE	23
THE DAY AFTER	24
ROUND CUBICLE	25
A DYING SEASON	26
THE RIDE	27
THE ROCK GARDEN	28
MOONLESS DAY	29
KINGDOM OF LOVE	30
EYES OF HORUS	31
HAPPY DIE DAY	32
OIL AND WATER	33
LIMBO	34
IDIOCY	35
SILENCE	36
PAINTING YOUR PORTRAIT	37
PHOENIX RISEN	38
Q	39
MY BELOVED MONSTER	40
WINTER ANGEL	41
GANDALF	42
HOLOGRAM	43
WHITE IS A DARK COLOR	44
CHAIN BREAK	45
THE SCENT OF YOU	46
TRUCE	47
YIN YANG	48
LOVESICK	49

MEDAL OF GRIEF	50
PARADISE LEAK	51
RESTING ON THE MOON	52
RAINBOW LOVERS	53
IGNORANCE IS BLISS	54
NIGHTWISH	55
MELTDOWN	56
DOOMSDAY	57
INSOMNIA	58
LOVELY DARK	59
ABOUT A DREAM	60
THE DEVIL IN DISGUISE	61
SPARK REVEALED	62
INFINITY	63
ENCHANTMENT	64
MY PERSONAL DRUG	65
TRAPPED BEAUTY	66
TACHYCARDIA	67
I SURRENDER	68
MY FAMOUS LAST WORDS	69

IVANA KOROVESOVSKA

It's **6 AM**.

I'm standing on a **GOLDEN MOUNTAINTOP**, trying hard to **HANG ON** and **HOLD STILL** to
find a **LIGHT IN THE DARK**...
WALKING DEAD all around me and my **VOLCANIC DREAMS** take
a **SIP OF THE HEART** and hang it on **THE APPLE TREE THE DAY AFTER**.
How did I end up in this
ROUND CUBICLE on **A DYING SEASON** while **THE RIDE** to **THE ROCK GARDEN** was instead a
MOONLESS DAY in a **KINGDOM OF LOVE**!
With **EYES OF HORUS** I watch my **HAPPY DIE DAY** turn into
OIL AND WATER, and I wish for **LIMBO** to switch places with this **IDIOCY**!

SILENCE while **PAINTING YOUR PORTRAIT** made me feel like **PHOENIX RISEN**,
with a simple **Q** in mind:
Does **MY BELOVED MONSTER** holds a **WINTER ANGEL** and plays **GANDALF**
on me, or is it just a **HOLOGRAM** telling me
that **WHITE IS A DARK COLOR**?

I hear a **CHAIN BREAK** whenever I feel **THE SCENT OF YOU**...

TRUCE taking place between **YIN YANG**, and only the **LOVESICK** can bear
to hold the
MEDAL OF GRIEF and
take it where the **PARADISE LEAK**!

RESTING ON THE MOON - three **RAINBOW LOVERS** who do not
care that **IGNORANCE IS BLISS**!

Make me a **NIGHTWISH** in this **MELTDOWN** on a **DOOMSDAY**, for I
suffer from **INSOMNIA** in the **LOVELY DARK**!

All I can say **ABOUT A DREAM** stolen from **THE DEVIL IN DISGUISE** is that
a **SPARK REVEALED**. **INFINITY** next to **ENCHANTMENT** are together **MY PERSONAL DRUG**,
hidden under **TRAPPED BEAUTY** slowing down my **TACHYCARDIA**.

I SURRENDER
MY FAMOUS LAST WORDS
to you...

IVANA KOROVESOVSKA

6 AM

Time and time again
for as long as I endure the minutes
passing rapidly cutting edge,
striking the exact hour of shocking hilarity
mesmerized by thrill and sincerity
while seconds of serenity
dwell like a lightning bolt
shining brighter than itself!

>Feel the bruises left undone
steering to make a patch
of what I use to hurt for,
and think not of the damage
feeding the pain trapped between.

Fill me the extra footage
as I stay tuned with excitement
making scenery come to live
and you fall right back into my wishing well
making a splat I'd never forget.

>Time freezes,
doesn't it baby?

>Make a wish for yourself as well,
I will find the coin and make it golden and real.
Tick-tack, Tick-tack...

The clock is a wretched device, sealed with a frame rate collapsing my tendency to endure precious moments I never even dreamed of. Vacant hours I never used, are a blissful joker I hold down my imaginary sleeve, and you take my clothes away every time you say goodbye...If only I had a magic wand to banish all the clocks in the city to a place never to be. Misbalanced and free, forever with me...

ME, MYSELF, AND IVANA

GOLDEN MOUNTAINTOP

How extraordinary the blue
painted on the summer skies,
turning a twinge into oblivion.

> Naked soul
> and all I feel is shivers down my heart...

Look,
above the meekness of my affection:
my very own separation from the inner-self,
rising with the speed of a snail,
crawling its way
to outlast the miracle of existence!

> And is it not you
> who consents my endurance?

> Wind cover,
> running thru our bare essence
> while the spirits hang their coats on my shoulder.

In the land of my 7-th heaven,
I welcome them to stay
in definite!

> Do you dare to share
> a piece of this soul,
> slipping away from all behind?

> Throw me the courage
> and we'll fly in the depths this collision
> holding my head up in the clouds.
> Join me, will you?

No matter the thrill, or the loving breath I take each time I stand next to you, you only hear a broken violin playing for the sake of music killing time. My hopes buried in the sun, and you caress me with the wind covering my warmth...Can't you hear the strings thru my heart's ears?

IVANA KOROVESOVSKA

HANG ON

Killing the element of child
rids you the blemish of fault
while I'm restless on the doorstep
waiting for a cry of a ring.
For as long as I'm lasting
tall but firm hanging on a limb
I wish for a moment of integrity
I lay upon the lurking below,
and minutes last for days
'cause I hang onto each second
you promised to grant me,
leaving me hopelessly exhausted
of the invented redemption finger aid.
Nonetheless the time trial
dictating every act of sympathy,
I beg of you to send me glance
saying that you to go by from time to time
just to spit on the past
clearly worthless in your memory,
though it witnesses my expiring breath
spreading rapidly like a virus
deadly to the weak and poor
surrounding my air space
dancing when harmony is at sleep.
Come around if you will,
and sell me one hand wave
so I can drop heavily
with ease...

For as long as I can take it – please do as I you will! I shall not cry to the killer taking my tears. I shall not refuse a deadly offer you intend to give away just to see if you could get away with it! I will not tell you to hide your claws! I love your wicked essence, but in return I wish you hate me for that!

ME, MYSELF, AND IVANA

HOLD STILL

As long as the shadow remains silent
I shall lift my inner spirit
to cast a ravishing spell in reverse
to set my desire at rest!
It is I alone stealing your sanctity
making me ill and grotesque
while every single monster
laughs at my beloved nightmare at the time being.
Don't ever stop and question
what is the price for my despair,
for it is painted in my voice of reason I long lost,
and I sing for the guilty at heart
purchased with a tune,
printed in anguish
posted to shock the entrenched
with a single hope for what I always felt was rightfully right...
How do you resist a screaming loner
begging for a soul to redeem,
while longing shapes essential purity
setting my spirit to run clean?
Separation is fatal to the fearful
since I never knew how to let go,
simply 'cause I never wanted to...
Killer without a victim
versus lover forever!
Falling harder...

When I reach the heavens above, you steal a piece of my heart holding your very own. I find the leftovers hidden in the dawn while you try to gather yourself, and I know not of what remains of you after me...While I count the shapes forming my endless nights, I write my vows and keep them safe within the dawning of every new day. I long for the moment I speak to the sun about how the moon cast the spell of affection, growing bigger and stronger! Will the two of them meet to see what they've done to me?

IVANA KOROVESOVSKA

LIGHT IN THE DARK

And as the hour of heart strikes,
I draw the strings tighter with fright
while you swing around
like a warm summer breeze.

                                  I forget about what is
                  so that midnight could steal my guts
                        and I let me be what I am.

Ice covers your burning flesh
while I shiver with burning desire
to feel your naked soul
and steal your passion of a silent scream.

                Filthy the thief lurking around
                      with a warning sign
              trying to lure the thirsty reverted!

                                      I hold my ground
                while glass carves a fountain of red
                      and I feel nothing but delight
                      since I felt you appending.

Even with morning rick,
I tend to collapse my horror of existence
and take the grayish blue
and color it gold...

                    Welcome to my world!

Rebirth from a different point of view. World collapsing, but suddenly a small token of pleasure, so significant and worthy of waiting, that I simply cross the borders of darkness without opening eyes. Can there be another so much like oneself? And then my clock stops, and I lose all track of what never mattered...I hear colors and paint the minutes with music...Who sent you? Unique and fragile...Slowly appearing...Forgetting...I become myself...

ME, MYSELF, AND IVANA

WALKING DEAD

Disclaim and praise the visceral
for it is the vintage of existence
identified by the fairly hearted,
blinded for the sake of what is.

Bow to the ignorant
blessed with each other's presence,
worthy of a body united!

Slowly,
I make peace with my longing
pulling me straight to agony,
and how I snivel for your silent ease
from a time everlasting,
locking me away
and shredding my up-comings scattered to pieces
ever since I last saw you.

Was it not you
that valued my heart willing to bleed
in order to receive a single spark of hope
killing me naked in the cold?

I laugh in the face of forgiveness,
resurrecting me to a place I'm no longer to be,
and I know you wait for me
every time you hear my teardrops
flooding my heavens on Earth…

Missing is the worst of all sins! Whenever you start missing the one person you want to see, sit yourself down and find a way to suffocate the crime of malevolence. The penalty is a lifetime of misery and anticipation that one sad little day the same person will eventually feel the same way and you will not care anymore! Why waste a lifetime in prison while the sun shines behind the bars of discourage? Unlock your shame and let go of the silly moment of absence, for it is time you act upon the days to be…

IVANA KOROVESOVSKA

VOLCANIC DREAMS

Warm breath
spread in the arms of a stranger
melting what can't be broken.
Scattered pieces fill a gap in my soul
made of fire and denial,
bruising the envelope
making its way deep within.
Rejected by shelter,
refusing embrace,
touched by stone and dinosaur...
When the world turns the sea against the wind,
if rain melts the sun's existence,
shall I witness your decency then?!
Will the light in our departure souls
crash the sin lurking from the pain you've caused?
Fading are memories
holding my bright and useless future.
And yet I cannot see behind walls,
put together by a startled friendly child.
The blindfold is a window of events
locking long lost and dead.
Dark clouds and injured ground,
Does no one have anything to say?

Fly among the gentle heat of the fire melting my heavens on Earth, and dwell inside just to spite the grotesque. And beware: the truth will set one free if one has the dignity to swim out from the lava of every day's eruption! Blow a kiss to the innocent while they scatter their love to the guilty and depraved, only to obtain moral stability. Isn't THAT marvelous?

ME, MYSELF, AND IVANA

A SIP OF THE HEART

As long as the infatuations dissolve
no matter how tight I tend to hang on
the grouch inside continues to evolve
draining the scraps left for gone.

> I look ahead with my head down
> and even though we eventually meet
> I hope you don't mistake me for a clown.

Honesty made my loved ones think
that I hold nothing but severity,
so I stand with a cup of drink
poured out to be true rarity
from my own finest pink.

> Whether you spill it or give it away
> I dare not ask you to stay
> since the sap lasts for only a day
> or so they use to say.

I close my eyes as I withstand the test
and feel nothing in my head
just a complete urge to finally rest
and lay this corps on a solid bed.

> I looked the second I stroke the ground
> and jolly hit the floor
> falling in love with sound
> feeling I as well owned somewhat of a core...

For as long as profoundness fails to find interest in amusement, the heart will not know of its true value. I step closer to the edge of desire as I laugh in the face of lust and passion! They sit next to each other, holding hands, blocking every single affection everlasting in ease! Make me a proud fool, and let me kill them all together! Can you crown the leftovers?

IVANA KOROVESOVSKA

THE APPLE TREE

Boundaries of leisure,
feelings buried in my backyard
hiding in the act of seizure,
with devil and his crossbar as guard
remote me from the hell I fell in love,
vigorously without any doubt,
frightened and disarmed like dove,
standing weedy with a crying shout.
When everything was simple and plain,
I couldn't make out the picture
and yet I withstand the drain
failing to ignore the structure.
I sat next to Sentinel
wrapped in dread of depression.
I decided to speak
to a language unknown
fluent without a leak
with dismissal to postpone.
In order to redeem my autonomy,
nonsense made me think that I made a deal
with the outrageous leader of the colony
brought from beneath to explain and reveal
of all that is buried and can only be released
outcoming with unusual shape
if one stands alone for the increase
willing to wear an everlasting cape.
My, what a lovely backyard it is...

In the misty nights when nobody is around, a craving for a forbidden fruit...Up there, hanging on a tree so dark and rotten it makes you sick just by looking! But yet, so lovely the red glow lighting the fog surrounding all. Dare to try the poisoned treat???

ME, MYSELF, AND IVANA

THE DAY AFTER

Step slightly within the trap
arrest your being for a little while
then I'll pull out the secret map
and replace a misfortunate expression with a smile.

Enfold your binding freedom aside
shouldn't that be a trophy to win?

Trick me to escape the hide
in order to commit the original sin.

Lure every hero inside of me
to come running with enlarging haste
and let each one to see
that their attendance is not at waste.

The one who will bite the chain
with a single swing of my soul,
will allow the spring to outlast the rain
and build us a tomorrow behind the nasty wall.

For whatever is worth in me
you will only bear a burden of blind hope
setting all your wicked spirits to be free
creating a path for our essence to slowly elope.

"Once you find your way to me, there is no turning back..."

IVANA KOROVESOVSKA

ROUND CUBICLE

Strings attached only to obtain
oppressive bond of a different vein
uprising in a virtual reality
while bruising the pragmatic totality.
Visual lies and psychotic truth
make me consider ever leaving the booth,
so comforting and absurdly small
growing intensely on top of it all.
Space converted in thoughts,
mildly connected with loosen knots
so the bandage works both ways
as the question yet remains:
Will it sustain the brightness of later days?
Never hesitate to honor the plain
for the sake of a superior gain
since everything will come to an ending
and ultimately once again be ascending.
Long live the secrets holding my back!

Firm water, runny sunsets and freezing looks. All of the sudden I realize that nothing is what it seems. My insides cry for my eternal truth to make its way to the outer! Can there be a rising event arousing everyone to reconsider their outlook? For the sake of beauty, dare to look with the heart made of sugar, resting on the red moon. It holds gently to every dream casted by the dreamers. Swallow the vision and endure the sight...

ME, MYSELF, AND IVANA

A DYING SEASON

Steal my warmth
and I'll reward you with gentle murder
committed for the honest and righteous
to continue their petty journey
to your deceiving heart.
Each and every time
I die little by little
watching you suffer while I sob,
enduring my passionate nature
eating my complete existence.
Only if for a night
on a passing dead beloved!
Break me if you will
and I shall pick up my expired pieces
only to laugh at your actions,
pointing a single act of gratitude
of a poor recital sang with a sound of a soul.
Isn't this enough?
Aren't you content with the vengeance?
Sleep tight until you come back
'cause I'm waiting for your arrival...

There comes a time when a season dies. The lovely snow melts the cover of spring, blooming intensely while the sun reaches highest summer point, drying off heavy leafs , when fallen await for the icy coat once again...Cycle of everlasting circles! Why does each season leaves something behind? Marks of a period coming to turns, over and over again...And never the same leaf touching the ground...

IVANA KOROVESOVSKA

THE RIDE

Freshness of an evening glance,
light soft breeze making me smile,
as I fall even harder
when you present me
your sweet fear of touches,
so I wouldn't brake.
Still as a summer night
warming precious moments
when something out of nothing
makes us forget everything else.
I steal a stare
while the melody plays
next to my depriving heart,
I pinch myself to believe
that you are
living,
current,
by my side...
If you embrace me I'm yours,
If you feel me I'm real.
If you love me I won't believe anything else...
I would like to stay.

Even with a drop of hope, I find ways to awake my soul in someone else's presence. It's the pieces you give away that always stay in your precious memory, forming a lovely image of what true affection looks like. Surrounded with tempting notes of what I call a "night to remember" I simply stop and stare at the city I once knew but no longer recognize. How far can a car go if you put it in idle? I'd say ALL THE WAY...
(For Michael)

ME, MYSELF, AND IVANA

THE ROCK GARDEN

With a gentle swing of a slow fade
made utterly of enticing everlast,
I hold my benevolent self next to all left undone
with a tendency to lose faith in all evil.

                                            Floating somewhere between us
                                            I forget about what's between us
                                as you start to unravel my forever and now
                                              fastening a stronger bond
                                                than you could imagine.

                            Can there be a different place
                                  holding us back in line,
              where I can have a glimpse of that ember you bestow?

I'm stealing a ray
never meant to warm a smile
I wanted to give away
without wrinkling my tattered soul...

                                                  The rock becomes dust!
                              Make way for the wind to take charge
                              and blow it back to my land of birth,
                              'cause all I ever hope and pray upon
                              is written in the depths of creation.

Never charged with a deed
so blissful and dishonest
but better yet I serve the sentence of delusion
setting my hell on fire...

                          Beware of the screaming silence called fact!

How tough a stone can get? I look beyond the rigid structure and smile for the sake of strength inside a hard rock minding its dues. Tossed and turned, blown and burned, it never settles to scream for submission to the frail! And somewhere along, a hand reaches out...It moves the pieces holding its ground, and by the time it soothes a shift of inevitability, the firm structure closes a deal of fate: what good a stiff outer if one has an empty core?

IVANA KOROVESOVSKA

MOONLESS DAY

With a cry of a smile
I shut the devil's eye
leaving my bare soul naked as it was.
Mistakes of a doubtful spirit
never taking good for granted!
You charged by the hour
as I dreamt of your loving arms.
Overwhelmed and delusional
I paid with pieces of a heart that broke,
and my wealthy essence
amused your darkness of existence
wrapping your aberrant whole.
Rest with me for a while...
Never mind the cold,
the filthiness,
the hideous background
or my lack of immorality,
for I still measure my time
from that single moment of resurrection
and somewhere in the valley of my thoughts
I see your beauty of deceit
with a smile of a cry
caressing the blind angel
that brought me to you...

I look up, and I see a den of stars, forming constellations of sparks, lasting a minute or two...Deranged by vision and mind, I blow directly at them with a blind hope that it might move the space between to make room for something different, something more like the light ball lighting my shadow of existence, each and every time I forget about the stars...

ME, MYSELF, AND IVANA

KINGDOM OF LOVE

Realm of desires,
coherent worlds beyond fantasy
where is thy ruler of existence
announcing enticing lust
spreading the sound of only what others heard.
A melody of false impression
concluding corruption
conceived from elegance of mind.
Permanent residence
for the diminished and sacredly frightened
forever let loose with ravishing courage
hastening to what is betrothed
in order to complete sought
and remain unforgotten.
Seal a devil's deal of hope and despair
of what once was taken
wanting to be owned by the rightfully righteous.
Who is to determine such destiny?
Blaming the blameless,
is everything an individual is left with
when not able to understand
the hierarchy of what is loved and detested
by whom we cherish and never accept.
Throw away the ropes holding one another to oblivion,
blindfolded,
rousing towards pleasure
and the fall of the monarchy!

Since the very beginning of time, the bounding of the opposites stands erect, and holds both ends in a never ending circle of continuance. Who is to say what opposes a single being in order to endure oneself and seeks for a whole other meaning by itself? Is it not that every flower has a different name and connects in a unique way to every living thing in this Earth that we know of, and yet holds all beauty for those brave enough to step closer? Blooming is a feature that can set a soul on fire...
Think about that!

IVANA KOROVESOVSKA

EYES OF HORUS

Wise is the one sitting in the dark
rising for the purpose of grand denial
subverting self at a single cause
never to retrieve for the sake of misery.

                              Some say that lunatic is made
                          out of anguish and embarrassment,
                         but the truth lies underneath
              to abide the laws of time and destiny itself.

Throw the riches in the dense,
care to beg for some more?

                               As the vision fades away
                      I see how the shallow and incomplete
                        make their dues to leave a mark
                   and set my demons without charge
                        in a place where I never existed
                           but all and sundry heard of
        about an underdeveloped and desolate creature
               ongoing only to set the wicked straight.

Unkind and weary,
I cry each time a wrong is made right
as I leave a death sign behind
as a witness to a deed
I wish not...

            May all of you rest in pieces!

Cursed is the one gifted with pleasure of a vision withstanding every right for wrong. Somewhere along the path of righteousness, I stop and look to my left. All I see is a startled child, reaching both hands, and on my right – an old woman, already holding my hand. I pick the little child up, while grandma sticks like glue. 6 legs, 6 arms, and only 2 pairs of eyes...I long for rest...

ME, MYSELF, AND IVANA

HAPPY DIE-DAY

Railway to freedom
while nighttime steals my wings of surrender.

I carry the shine on a winter's day
proudly searching for my inner voice
screaming loners sacrificial choice
stuck between a "want" and a "may".

Wandering hasted around a dying city
wrapped around my 24 karat love,
I see you waiting with a light of a soul
and then you ask me to deny
my right to suffer in worship.

Shiver all you want!

My aching side cannot bare my truth
since the heart shines brighter than the Moon
and I look at you,
finishing your cigarette of a dream
blowing at the candles
as they burn the moment away.

When you took my treasure,
did you stop to think
with what am I left to measure
the reason that passionately sinks
under your lies colored in pink?

It's a shame you missed that train...

The moment you start looking through the eyes of your heart, you discover a new world. Some might say that deeds speak louder than words, but what if you merge them all together? What if the reason we are gifted to speak our hearts out, finally makes a difference for non-other than ourselves? One's boldness lays in determination to go the distance, but my own settles the hardest question: What if I go beyond? And I did ☺ I took the train to my Loveland and I met myself along the way. It's a one way ticket...And I enjoy every single minute of it!

IVANA KOROVESOVSKA

OIL & WATER

Reason and rhyme
truth and crime,
hollow and shallow
green with serene
all can come together
and stay there forever.
Crisp the cradle by the dangle
rock the virtue by its handle
dare for some more
or shall we meet to adore?
I want to go where wilderness gives warm welcome
you desire to stay where deer rest.
Mix and match
fire and flames
do you crave to catch
what no man blames?
Keen to make amends
you speak of a different time,
so place them demands,
for me to straighten the line.
Cruel is the one who is shocked with worship
and refuses to say without bearing in mind
moving with the speed of a starship
to the unknown to become primed.
Effortless and clean,
slash and mildly obscene
rousing toward primacy
you tend to collapse excitedly
to what I use to think made my heart puny
and by men nowadays considered gloomy.
Some things are better left unfelt...

If only the heart could age as well as the body of a person...Life would be a different story!

ME, MYSELF, AND IVANA

LIMBO

It's the shallow drifters that linger at most
and my naked soul weeps for the effort
when I come across the simplicity of a sensation
written on their filthy backs.
Mistaken and sealed by the wretched,
I make peace with a single hope of a recollection
about strong passions conceived with adultery
creating a mess in my pinkish utopia
while everything coexists for a different cause
and I forget about what I long for...
Out of the blue,
you craft my ease with a single blink
making me feel the unfelt and long forgotten
while all the rest ceases to lose importance
and by the time you open your eyes
I become a bit more than myself.
Will I not redeem a guilty state of heart
for the sake of surrender?
The handcuffs slowly brake
and I will not resist the escape
although I've never been to the land in-between,
but since thy arrival
fear turned me into a fast runner
and I run only to make you feel my haste
sweeping you off your reason and mind.
Close those eyes and dream for a while...

Stuck in the middle of the good and not so good. The time when my power of will overcomes my power to submit to the only truth ever taken for granted is now! I struggle to convey a survey about a past eating my guts in order to step further and never make a similar notion in the times to be. Can a person of such learn the concept of letting go has a larger impact than holding back? Water stays clear even if it changes course, so I become the course instead. Pure was an option long before the course took action, and I had to switch roles.

IVANA KOROVESOVSKA

IDIOCY

Coward is the one
sitting in the light of day
singing along with birds
depriving the cheerless and tarnished.

If I craze
will you forgive me?

So do tell about your wrongdoings
and I'll redeem my fortune
fooling your sense of wisdom.

Marvelous isn't it?

Vicars and angels
fall at my feet to induce me
to mourn for their purpose.
I stand alone when I speak of you
and then I deny their being again.

How is it that something measured for less,
can make you ride rainbows to heaven?

Incline me the right to care
and I'll stay forever.

I cry only with the rain
and still they count my every teardrop
as if it was meant to drown the wellness
for I suffer only to stand in line
and bow t it!

Smile with me for the sake of tenderness!

Crippled by the cripples, I made peace with my dues of a past long forsaken. Never stop to look back at the chains once holding your back! Lose yourself in the freedom binding your fortune while your heart sets the time right. Crying for what's long gone, can always cast a joyful cheer for what awaits! As my aching soul rests, I hear a buzzer reminding me of the moment that is now! ENJOY!

ME, MYSELF, AND IVANA

SILENCE

Vicious virtue,
is there a similar meaning to what is behold?

>   Plain and not so simple,
>   I wonder how the truth is involved...

How is it that the red can turn into stone,
betrayal can vague the discomfort from the wind
carving scars all over the unsaid,
making life's necessities unpleasantly grind!

>   Thru the magic of youth
>   we eek comfort in the undone,
>   just to become something out of the one thing that is truly ours...

>   So what makes a running man faster?
>   Why do the leaves leave their creator?
>   When the sun meets the moon,
>   you will see me rising from the dirt
>   luring my way to vengeance soon,
>   chasing away purity in everlasting circles!

Forgiveness is inevitable in the state of abandonment,
and then a single soul can tell that the light is warm...

Whenever a wordless conversation sets place, I stop to think: what if I painted with my eyes closed? Would the picture than lose all meaning and value? Touched by the soul's inner voice, I tend to recollect all that is written deep inside, and sing it thru the beautiful sound of a human heart! Why should one have doubts about a profound meaning of what is truly felt? Fairytales and dreamlands exist if one has courage to admit the devil lurks behind, silently, to demoralize the meaning of all fair and treasured, and I set the time he comes in the scenario!

IVANA KOROVESOVSKA

PAINTING YOUR PORTRAIT

Heavy rain dropping hard
and I hardly see you.

The sound of your wet hair
covers my eyes
as I struggle not to touch you.

I remember loving the sun,
and melt away by your side.
Hands move without control...

```
,,,,,,,,,,,@,,,,,,,,,,,,,,,,@,,,@
,,,,,,,,,@,@,,@,@,,@,,,,@
,,,,,,,@,,,,,,,,,,,@,,,,,,,,,,,@
,,,,,,,@,,,,,,,,,,,@,,,,@,,@
,,,,,,,,@,,,,,,,,, ,,,,@@,,@
,,,,,,,,,,@,,,,,,,,,,,,,@,,,@
,,,,,,,,,,,@,,,,,,,,,,,@,,, @
,,,,,,,,,,,,,,,,,@,,,,,,,@,,@
,,,,,,,,,,,,,,,,,,,,,,@,,@
,,From,,,,,,,,,,,,,,,@
,,,,,♥,,,,,,,,,,,,,,,,,,,,@
,,,,,,,,,,to,,,,,,,,,,,,,,@
,,,,,,,,,,,,,,,♥,,,,,,,,,,@,,,,,@@@
,,,,,@@@@,,@,,,,@,,,,,,,,,,,@
,,,@,,,,,,,,,,,,,,@@@,,,,,,,@@
,,,,,,@@@,,,,,,,,@,,,@@
,,,,,,,,,,,,,,,,,,,,,,,,,,@
,,,,,,,,,,,,,,,,,,,,,,,,,,,,@
,,,,,,,,,,,,,,,,,,,,,,,,,,,,@
,,,,,,,,,,,,,,,,,,,,,,,,,,,,@
,,,,,,,,,,,,,,,,,,,,,,,,,,@
,,,,,,,,,,,,,,,,,,,,,,,,,,,@
,,,,,,,,,,,,,,,,,,,,,,,,,,,,,@
```

For as long as I remember...

ME, MYSELF, AND IVANA

PHOENIX RISEN

In for the kill
among the living dull
striving for a drop of wisdom,
where supreme takes over all
and the only one standing
is yourself and you.
Reason and evil make peace
and I wonder how far am I supposed to get,
to outlast insanity
trapping my demon of lust.
Sad is the wind
running around to blow my piece of mind,
while you run In circles
surrounding my nature of wealth...
You hold onto a bottom of a dream
mistaken every action for deed!
Whistle to the deaf
but never laugh at the one-eyed person
crying to you,
since you only see in the light of day
while darkness sets the hour of truth!
Beware...

If the dead could speak...Isn't the silence louder than the eviction? Bring the evicted further to keep quiet while the mouth whispers last breath of blind prayers for the crippled to remember: Once there was a walking deaf, with a single eye in function, and he couldn't speak of the scavenger stealing what he once owned and now only obsesses about...Remains of a sight nearly left for gone, but better yet – a window still not broken ☺

IVANA KOROVESOVSKA

Q

As you stumble thru the surface do you twirl?

When you see perfection do you set aside all effort?

How deep are your seas?

Is my soul's transparency making it invisible?

How come we ache for the lost and refuse to forget?

Are all humanoids sadistic?

Why do you hold back from beauty?

Why the sun makes me think of your pale skin?

Can you turn the world around?

Can you turn my world around?

Would you?

Try?

Do you ever wonder why we wonder?

ME, MYSELF, AND IVANA

MY BELOVED MONSTER

Finally I'm in love,
with your absence and nothingness
not only by spite and devotion
will I be able to fling relic of nil,
and rid the gash mortifying my whole.
Finally I'm in love
with not missing an opportunity of such,
to demolish a creature naïve,
giving you days yet to become,
to you almost not be worthy of.
Finally I'm in love
with a choice
of affection only surviving on fright,
a heaven
where demons feed on poor keepers of good,
a life
that only I could give you
and I did,
despite you leaving it to the worthless
without shame
making me surrender my life form to them...
I despise the ground you step on,
I envy the air surrounding you,
I cry for the bed you lay every moonrise,
I suffocate when I can't breathe you,
I mourn for my doom,
just to ask:
what gave you the nerve to harm yourself?

Praise the stillness of sound surrounding my inner frenzy. It is the hungry for vengeance lurking around my deaf heart to strip the soul only to laugh at the tears holding my essence! Shame on them for not knowing the truth! As long as I bear my burden of existence I shall not stand behind a wall of disgust, just to redeem a shameless sinner...Behold – I am what I've always been!

IVANA KOROVESOVSKA

WINTER ANGEL

On a white night
by a chocolate bench
I'll be waiting in vain
holding my ground
until it cracks open.

                              The beam screaming to break
                                        as I watch closely,
                     anticipating my apocalypse of heart
                                  setting soul on fire
                           with every beat of my breath.

Night creatures hiding among clouds,
what happens in a blink of an eye
while we rest in the dark shades
away from daylight?

                              Streams of beauty run thru me
                                        for one last time
      and I shut my senses to the rest of my feelings.
                      I'm guilty for the black feathers
                                     covering my back.

I apologize for what you've done to yourself...

There I was. Standing, with a warm heart, and freezing cold hands. Snow falling with ease. I'm waiting for a thunder in a wrong season to strike my conscience! Silence and ease take over my being, and I pray for mercy from heaven. It's getting colder...Darker...I see this bench calling out to me. I sit down and I look at the winter sky melting my heart away...I float with every snowflake...

ME, MYSELF, AND IVANA

GANDALF

Nasty magician is playing a trick on me.
Do I like it?
I seem to buy the filthy scam.
Does he even care?
Dreams and illusions take over the moment.
Where am I?
Flowers and stars made of nothing.
What has become?
Flying delusional deception seizes control.
Who am I?
None other than the spiteful,
smutty,
despised by none other than myself.
ILLUSIONIST...

Once a human mind expands, it never tends to come back to its original size. Once you feel your heart connecting to that expansion, the world becomes a fairytale where you float endlessly and all the little people underneath smile when looking at you. Want to stay there forever? Off course! Rainbow skies and sunny nights, while everything and everybody goes down under and you seem to not care. But the fall is inevitable, since the flight lasts for a while...Wake up and smell the thorns and remember, if there is no moon – the stars wouldn't care if they shine or not!

IVANA KOROVESOVSKA

HOLOGRAM

Falling stars all night long
brighten up a lonely expression
shadowing a possible loss of adventure
proudly sneaking up behind me
setting off to a place where I'm not.
Each and every dark hour,
lasts a bit longer than eternity
with thoughts undone
chasing inside my crazed head like
dog, cat and their best friend Jerry.
I watch slowly how you come across
smiling at them quietly
not to disturb my attention
even though I want nothing else
but the absolute contrary.
I feel nothing but an absent presence
of a beauty from my imagination
coming alive merely
thee inches away from me.
Then I reach out to touch you
when my heart stops
as you vanish faster than the shooting stars,
just in time for me
to wish you well...

Yearn for the image inside a head full of itself, before you lean to the remains of what makes you perfectly sane! Madness dwells in my blood, but I never contaminate another...if my lunacy is called pure affection will you join me in a mad house of adore? Too little, too late...

WHITE IS A DARK COLOR...

Long is the path to truthfulness
grieving my consent to the finish,
but lay back and take pleasure by the hand
running boldly to catch a flame,
while glory is painted by memory,
beauty is conceived with time
marching side by side,
laughing in the face of all you cherish,
crying behind the back of all I detest.
Wait for me in white
even if I'm not suited for thee.
Be there just to calm my mad heart,
and I promise to leave you.
Bring me to the self I once loved
in order to open a door
and banish all my miseries from heaven
straight to the other place
where I can't feel you anymore.
Fairytales and dreamlands,
hear me roar:
WHERE IS THAT WORLD DIVINE?!

http://www.youtube.com/watch?v=YKIWZxB_d0E

IVANA KOROVESOVSKA

CHAIN BREAK

Why is the grim subtler than the honest?
Slow the voyage from what is there,
to what is truly ours to grant.
Bleak be the superior telling us different,
about a singular choice
of affection over mindful existence.
Mists covering the consideration
about standing still
when the urge makes a crying wish
of the condemned to take pleasure!
And somewhere along,
a hand riches as a reminder
to what is beneath the sand of disbelief
holding your chains by the throat,
as you unleash the creature of fervor
raging against what the terror.
Make way for the uprising!
The millennium counts every minute in despair
while my hopes and dreams live for tomorrow
and I smile to the future
where I can see you shine brighter
with each passing heartbeat
heard by none other
than the one making it faster…
Bloom away – it's your season!

For what it's worth in every single cell in every single creature, I stand to make a simple difference from the truth - to the essence of all the fabrication covering the full of one self. When the final hour becomes a gateway to the other world, will there be a trial for the worthy to up stand all the rest? I cry for the righteous and strong since the very day I felt righteousness and strength! And I smile to the rest…Throw my weak heart in a bank not worthy of robbery…

ME, MYSELF, AND IVANA

THE SCENT OF YOU

So the night became my land of birth
and I stared at the glitters until it aches,
from a gentle spot by your shoulder
leaning closely to feel innocence.

>I repeatedly ask myself
about a moment of truth everlasting
in a secret chamber of occasions
predestined to put us at rest
as we become rapidly involved
with fate of rapture.

A clean heart weakened with each thought
of a burden carrying the heaviest crime…

Step further,
enduring the weight I intend to bear
for as long as you pack it
and don't you dare shed a tear
about a wonderer moving the time's grip!

>Your enchanting fragrance,
fill my veins with poisonous hope
that someday you will look at the rear
without anger or disgust
thinking only of each other.

I adore you still…

A memory made of an aroma playing my senses to a point where I hold onto a flicker in the heart. Oh what a delightful torture it is! I inhale thee, and exhale a part of my soul captured and released by a moment of truth underlining my dreams about a dream I dream…What a lovely merger of a mind over fact! And yet I wonder: how can a remembrance be written in scent, and forgetfulness take a form of irrelevance?

IVANA KOROVESOVSKA

TRUCE

Put down the shields of fame,
surrender to the thorn roses!

Scent of blood,
smell of tranquility
that caress you throughout the day.

Take a ride on the sunset
make a prisoner out of me
as if I don't like to be a captive of the innocent
leaving you restless and comforted.

Butterflies,
dancing even after death…
The flower ball is yet to come!

What you wanna do?

I don't care as long as I'm with you.
What if that were true?

As long as the fearless stand behind their protégé, the world will not know of silence beyond belief…
Spring in my soul, on a freezing night! Stand closer to feel a warm loner, for it is the light from within making the shine so lovely and bright. Dash inside the beauty to seize a ray of hope and delight made just for one…Remember to lock the door behind you…

ME, MYSELF, AND IVANA

YIN YANG

Rapture of delight
noise that brings my soul at ease
is what I grasp
whenever by whoever
mentioned thy being.

>At times I wish for somebody to hear
what can only be felt
and enlighten me that I am a con at heart
that only speaks of such bliss
when no one is around.

Black is the day
and white is the color pausing my absence.

>I look beneath the line of submission
and still wonder
if there is anything below,
and yet I dread to see
what I know only continues
in my head at night.

The Sixties wore plain clothes
and nowadays
everything is painted with disguise.

>The eye separates from the dead body
without fear of desertion.

Dark is the truth,
and vivid color is the penalty for my narration...

If the black lacks the white, the concept of truth over lie, mind over matter, would lose the pattern of good versus evil leaving the world as a hopeless den of bore. What if the sea wasn't made of water? Would you dare to swim in the unknown? Would you drink the sand from the desert to get to me? I hope not...Stay aware of the duality, that's worth living for!

IVANA KOROVESOVSKA

LOVESICK

Crawl underneath my bed
with presence I won't acknowledge
till the moment I dream of your joyful face
and you wake me with delight
originated of gladness same
as the night before
and the night after.
Haunt me when I'm aware,
wondering straight into my 3D,
so that I wouldn't stroll all alone and crazed
calling out your name
where no one cares if you are to be
or even not,
since I don't care if I'm mad
'cause I feel you in a state of reason
or even not.
My mental state of heart
is irrelevant at this point
as I seal my mind and slowly creep
to our asylum of discreet
forgetting of diagnose and routine
since we already locked the key in the middle
forever
and ever
and after that...

Unwell of the arousing sensation caused to make me ill of the promises made for a single night taking place in my mind. What a thrill, the world collapsing in a second, and all you do is sniffle covering your face! Reveal your sympathy as a token of weakness, and I shall not cry for your sins no more. The virus is taking the whole of me, and I have to be quarantined...Farewell!

ME, MYSELF, AND IVANA

MEDAL OF GRIEF

Prowl my innocence and pray for mercy
for I sleep only to scent you fading away...

                          Prime me your presence to breathe you forever
                                 as I turn away from the stink of my reality.

Take a deep long walk beside a drifter
born with a medal of a friendly doom
engraved forever,
invisible to the blind
but heavy to my beloved
as I crawl underneath my triumph of adversity over truth!

                     Would you share a single hand?

                                 Only to touch the shining misfortune
                                      honored by the cursed...

TAKE IT!
I cry for your tears endlessly...

Heavier than the Earth – I hang a prize on my neck to praise my lonely days to come. This is how a winner at heart should look like: clenched and deprived of all that enlightens fair outcomes about a dream not worthy for dismissal! I hold my ground only to stay aware of your existence...Will you cut me a piece of your precious time to think about what made me invisible to the rest while you stayed hidden behind me? Think for just a second. Thank you!

IVANA KOROVESOVSKA

PARADISE LEAK

The right to make amends
preserved to single.
Treason is universal language
spoken by the sinking in the deep
to sadly catch a string
covered with dirt.
In the depths of your darkness
am I the only switch
making you fall even harder?
When do I stand for myself
with all my ignorance and bliss,
resting on a sparkling dot
sitting on this bare chest?
The law abides the frail
and it all begins,
leaving the spotless den of dreams
buried in the heavy beyond...
Congratulations, you've lost!

If you see an injured doe, crying for a helping hand and you leave it helpless in the darkness of our memory, will it not haunt you till they burry your filthy corps?!

ME, MYSELF, AND IVANA

RESTING ON THE MOON

As I make my gateway
to the razor-sharp yellowish reflection
you point your half-open mouth
sighing.

As I feel your breath on the back of my heel
everlasting in motion
setting me back in time
anchoring my weakness,
never knew could sluggish me with immensity
of the black magic attached in a form of a parasite
growing inside out
slowly,
making me ill of the good I've made
but was never acknowledged.

I sit on the edge
with doubt it will ever crumble.
It draws me to exhaustion,
but I astonish myself
each and every time I light the warmth
originating from the distance between,
making my tiny core
shine upon without your accordance
and making me worry less
of the day you come across...

Drifting inside out while the night takes away the wings of surrender! I crawl naked to serve a moral goal and pay my ticket to a valuable existence, only to put aside all that has to be felt and not neglected, while the day takes its turn...Mourn for my ill being as I cross paths with the devil luring me to make a living among the dead! Warning signs only collapse in front of me, and I tire from silly attempts to keep walking beyond the ravel of the final chapter taking my whole.

IVANA KOROVESOVSKA

RAINBOW LOVERS

With one hand behind my back
I reach out to touch you
and I close my eyes rewinding the track
of all the things that we do
and suddenly everything is colorless and black
losing ground of hope and strength.
Life's chances
mirages...
Leading and misguiding
strapped from demon and heart.
Liberation of all miraculous,
create one beautiful lie
to bond all that I dream of
and can't imagine waking up without.
Squeeze my smiling face,
weaken me gently and slow
leaving afterwards with simplicity and grace,
just don't stand so helpful and low,
cause we are all the same race,
and all we have left is to grow...

Hand in hand, side by side, together forever until morality do us part! Make a witness of this time for worship, and we'll sail away to sign a contract of everlasting love. Steal the night with a swing of a soul as we swing along dancing the dance of devotion...Dare to venture?

ME, MYSELF, AND IVANA

IGNORANCE IS BLISS

Creepy the silence surrounding me
creating an eternal black sea
drowning my tender soul,
leaving nothing but a pallid hole.
Sometimes I fight the inevitable,
while soothed to stay focused and stable
so that all wrong would die out
and my aching heart could proudly shout:
What happened to that single drop of affection
leaning on my shoulders as a reflection
of a civilization long gone,
chasing all fair and innocent after midnight sun
on a sinister sub-zero weather,
where birds are deprived from feather
and every cry for a helping hand
is considered and ordeal or a withstand?
Prolong to suppress,
a basic instinct measured for less
to stay alive just one more day
for the jealous and envious to never say,
that a being never sacrificed time
to commit a mankind's major crime!

I can only look back with a smiling face, to the time where I first felt the sun hurting my skin, the snow freezing my poor little hand on a blizzard in the cold of the day. Those were the days to remember! All I hear now is rain...Falling down without any regret, and I never get wet! It never stops, but I love it for that...The constant pour makes me full of maturity and ease, and even though I pour along, nobody can ever see...

IVANA KOROVESOVSKA

NIGHTWISH

I wish upon a star at night,
so loneliness would stand further than you
and chain itself for good
just for my sake of forgiveness.
I wish upon a star at night,
to warm your weary expression
while the night is still young
and lay blinded right by your side.
I wish upon a star at night,
oh how I wish
someone could put an end of the night!
The cold,
the freezing bliss of that star,
making me beg for your fortune at heart
as I surrender my dreams
and you long for another,
worthy not for your light
but only your upcoming...
I wish upon a star,
to set your darkness on fire,
let you feel the heat of this burn
along with every feeling I ever had,
about a constellation of love
seen by the sightless
who only felt our soul's merger
for a second or two...
I wish upon a star,
to obtain my single right
since you hold my longings and I no longer yearn for anything but
freedom...
Good morning to me!

There lived the poor creatures, who only endured to the submission of a significant other. The giver becomes indulged with giving more, and forgets about asking to take a single recognition about all one did in order to close a cycle of completion, but never having to reach the peak of it! Life always stands for 3 simple things: respect, movement and selfishness! Can there be one without the other?

ME, MYSELF, AND IVANA

MELTDOWN

Why now?

Is it that all I treasure and seek
has lost content of use for me?

How come?

For the love of morality
when everything was enduring and plain
could it be that I did not see thee?
Sober my guilty need for purity!

Twist my knowledge into amusement of heart,
deceit me if you will,
just stand beside
and mistake my fear for lack of prudence
'cause I'm simply on my own
not to be with everyone else.

I've been decisive on soul bearing
one or too little times before
waiting for my back to break
to admit defeat
onto all I detest and dread upon
loosing the tiara of benevolence
given without resistance
in this farce of happening.

So seize me as I am,
since I was ultimately conceived
for none other than ourselves.

Measles they say, are very dangerous if caught later in life. Some say even deadly! I caught my measles age 24...Marks all over body, fevers and long-lasting nausea! It's not a very nice picture, especially when you hear that little voice in the back of your head: why didn't you sit next to that little girl back in '92 diagnosed with chicken pox? Oh well...Better late than never

IVANA KOROVESOVSKA

DOOMSDAY

I joy with the miserable
and sob with the pleased,
bitter yet along
the reminiscence erects
honoring insanity.
Only in my head
the astonishing twin lover lives on
comprehending my idea
set from a blood line
pure and poisonous
dripping constantly from this heart of mine.
Crowded this world
where the worthy rage against us.
I state now,
at 5 minutes to 12
as I make my way away:
Farewell my truthful hearted virtuous creatures!
The price you pay
is counted with each aching smile
for as long as you suffer with content,
'cause I admit my scars
and bow only to my weaknesses,
laughing in the rain
while my soul pours along…

Tic-tac, tic-tac…………BOOM!

ME, MYSELF, AND IVANA

INSOMNIA

Every time I want to scream you a whisper
I hear the night crawling up behind me,
stealing my soul's quiet voice
and my numbness is appreciated
where owl and starlight play hide and seek
creeping like thieves,
disturbing me senseless off my feet
in the precious moments
I agree upon your presence.
Wounds of silence,
grow deeper nurturing my anticipation
of the lie I tell myself
each and every time day covers darkness.
My reason and priceless sanity
make insomnia bearable,
postponing a nightmare of reunion
I wish and pray for
since the day you banished me away!
The night bird stopped playing the silly game,
since the Moon overshadowed the all-glittering.
I forgive you for the kill...

Close your eyes and sleep...Dream of all the beauty covering your senses with the tendency to sleep forever and crash your fears and doubts along the moonset and hopefully you'll sleep all through the morning, and the afternoon, so that night fools you to keep dreaming...With eyes closed I hear only stars scattering all over the dark-blue sky, and cannot rest. Dreams are gifts, and I was never gifted with a reason to stay away from my sleep...

IVANA KOROVESOVSKA

LOVELY DARK

Fetish or an easy object
I target my attention to,
while the world rumbles in flames
and you tend to apply a distinguisher
to all the heat melting my frozen insides,
I wonder,
what made you that special?

>   Blessed curse,
> setting my senses rage against my will
>   sharing my soul's inner peace
>   with all precious and unworthy of,
>   while you linger in darkness,
>   I wonder,
>   who made you that unique?

I crave for my surrender in the night
so that I feel shades taking a form of pleasure
surrounding our shelter of gloom,
shining only when moon rises above sun
and everything else makes sense
to the senseless lovers of doom,
vanishing along the vapor of lust
that I fell into for a single moment or two…

                WHERE ARE YOU?

My hands, guilty of caress! My heart, condemned with purity! MY soul, drifting slowly away…Darkness is not a color, only a lack of beauty shadowed by the unknown. Smile for the sake of never ending happiness, so that I close my eyes and remember only you in the mid black…

ME, MYSELF, AND IVANA

ABOUT A DREAM

Your body attached on my back
me losing all sanity to black,
as I feel your scent taking over me senseless
mesmerizing me utterly weak and fully restless.
I step outside myself to see
a childish grin I bestow myself for thee,
nailing me solid with no resistance
to a lucid shape in a mind of distance.
I never turn towards completely
as my strong motion deserts me discreetly
so I'm at my inclusive simplicity
launching our finishing form of spirit electricity.
Eyes are closed and sealed by an actual smile
and I dare you to make my heart compile
all the gleam surrounding us with delight
thus we float frivolously afar of sight.
Lifeless arms won't let loose
my only chance of this celestial seduce
for it is I alone creating a scene
of a vision originally unseen
yet to be sculpt
in order to be gulped
in a moment of sigh
before I even try
to tell myself
about the elf
poking me in the eye
without ever telling me why...

Lucid dreaming is a form of a miraculous rebirth I seem to encounter with, every time a reality is more appealing than a compulsory tiresome sleep. Ever since I am aware of what dwells in the second portion of my subconscious – as funny as it may sounds, I tend to dream in control and make a puppet out of myself, in order to set boundaries of leisure in a state of mind where I take the sun by the hand and tell it to rise from west! But every time the little man appears I remember that there is also a lovely moon, clearly neglected by the almighty me ☺
Live out the sun and moonrise! It's now or never...

IVANA KOROVESOVSKA

THE DEVIL IN DISGUISE

Devotion leaks.

>   Symbol of the time to be,
>   from the time that never was.

>   Share some will you?

Heroic attempt to outcome,
the never ending why
of a query unknown to mankind.

>   Was it not me who stood up for our beloved end?

>   Take it,
>   bare It,
>   throw it
>   or even share it!

Then madness shall rise from the ashes
to sweep you off your feet,
while I swallow your times of yore.

>   Sweet defeat,
>   stay hidden in the light of day
>   so that beauty survives the hell I created.

>   Suck it up,
>   it's all yours!

Masks underneath masks...A huge charade of hidden faces bruising my soul and making me sad in the broad daylight while my expression stays exposed! What to do among the unseen while every single one points and laughs at you? Leave? Or just join in? I say – leave!

ME, MYSELF, AND IVANA

SPARK REVEALED

Crippled and forsaken
flowing in an endless sky of disregard
I shall abide the pour just to stay on track
and redeem a condemned spirit by the hand.
Nightmare set loose in a land of callousness
where I've seeded my warmth
and you found comfort in the cold
embracing the frigid floor holding you tight,
just to spite my seldom nerve for dispute
about a friendly gesture of disgust
laid upon a sinking thrive
nurtured by one and all,
but myself...
How could I've known
the blue charade taking place in my very core
could sound peacefully honest?
How could I've outcome my childish star
left lonely in the up above
never reaching your love for bitterness?
Hear my shine
and remember the strong grasp of hope
I hold selfishly for thee
ever since I know you flush in the bleak of your den
every time you light my candle in the dark!

Temple of reminiscence, where all wicked lurks quietly to steal my perfectly imperfect outlook. I forget about who I am, and only see a tiny spark generated in the distance...I come closer, and when I reach out I touch a cold and flat surface signed with my reflection! I stare for a minute or two and blow straight into it so it would go off. It never does...

IVANA KOROVESOVSKA

INFINITY

As I step firmly
earth becomes den.
How I'd love to fall next to your dissolving flesh!
Misleading are the moments
mistaken as such.
Cry me a river of blood
and I will drown my indulging outlook
just to feel a piece of your body.
Naked and barefoot
full of desire...
Never doubt the taste of you
could sore as much
since my senses leave me
beside myself,
desperate for another addiction
to seduce my intentions
of what I must not deny.
Hate me or leave me,
for I don't care how belittle you think of me
'cause I sentenced myself
long before eternity!

I serve my severest penalty for an addiction made entirely of heart and longing. Mourn the beloved and crash the barrier pulling your guts by the hair, since no one will ever see the color pink thru those brownish eyes of yours...Fear me don't you? Don't hesitate to look again – I'm still looking at you through the glass, and although it is covered with dirt, I still feel the pain in your sigh, I still hear the turning of your head, trying to avoid the sadness in my heart...Hopefully I will leave the cell in pieces!

ME, MYSELF, AND IVANA

ENCHANTMENT

The sound of your shadow
walking away from magic in the night,
since the wand was blown away
and never coming to turns...
I stay lost between illusion and trick
and the moon steals my pleasure
like a thief from heaven,
sent only to laugh at the dark mirage!
Never enough...
Can I sweep a lovely creature off its feet
without injuring a spell of truth?
Cast me your dreams
and I shall banish the demon
standing in-between!
Crawl underneath the star cover
and stay a while,
just until forever makes me want for more...
Hex of desire
made entirely for a single soul
united with heart shades beating as one...
****

Carving a scenery inside a soul, clearer than pure water...It's the simple pleasure of the night alone overflowing the body in an endless sensation forming my celestial whole! The universal truth shouts my name along the tall green, surrounding my inner fury wasted early in the dawning of an era visible only to myself...And there you are, invisible and lovely...I can feel my presence beneath the darkness and hear only the sigh of your delight, narrating this abduction of a heart struggling to find its way to yourself! Can't there be a better version of this last couple of words?

IVANA KOROVESOVSKA

MY PERSONAL DRUG

Strike me your severest passion
and dwell with me for the sake of good fortune
while I cry for the weapons of desire
covered with blood and tears
bringing me to the darkest hour of our reality
right next to that lovely fear of touch and caress.

                              Play me a dying wish of hope
                    and I'll smile on behave of our damned misfortune
                              as we speak of the love forever to be
                    and let hold of the silly ties holding us together.

Crossroads marking a senseless track
circling around with the speed of a heartbeat
thumping with a love beat from hell
and I shake my diseased heart of its nonsense
while you step closer to the devil in me
and I have nothing left to give you
accept myself.

                                        Take me now
                              for I will never be as I am!

I swear I speak the truth
the whole truth
and nothing but the truth!

Addiction of lust, obsession over reason, craze for affection! Leave the broken behind as you let go of all strings pulling your senses below…Am I not worthy of attention? Were you the only one granting me the power of disobedience while I crawled at your feet calling your name? Will you remember me the day you can't remember anything else? The devil had spoken! AMEN!

ME, MYSELF, AND IVANA

TRAPPED BEAUTY

Endearing as you seem
I stand closer
completing a circle of beauty,
delicate and translucent
for it is only the protector
bestowed with undeniable pleasure
to feel a breath of a sigh
you charge overwhelming for.
So I made my way
to end this charade of forbid,
frantic to reach you
though I'm not worthy
of a single attempt,
since no one ever heard or seen
the entrance beneath your feet,
anchoring my friendless heart
seeking for true friendship
pondering inside your soul.
Let me enter...

Locked behind walls and gates, I grasp the doorman by the hand, asking the simplest question: why stand so still, guarding the stillness of another? The penalty for the crime is twice as appealing to the one sitting in the back! With a whisper of a soul, and a heart stronger than a rock, I cherish all the lovingness that carries me thru the hardness of what is to be...I hold a single hope by the hand, and sing to the birds for the freedom of a song kept away...

IVANA KOROVESOVSKA

TACHYCARDIA

Infatuated by the exquisiteness
on a cold wintery night,
overcome my trivial hesitation
to the unfelt desires of wrong.

I take a closer look
and yet can't tell the difference
whether reality fades,
or bows to imagination of will.

Simple as the falling slow,
melting my resistance of blast,
I hear nothing but a beating drum
bouncing in my hall of chest.

Stand slightly closer,
feel the tumbling performance from inside
for as long as you can bear,
and notice the beat gets heavier
whenever you try to outlast the gig.

I love the song without a name...

Some tunes are better left unheard. Whenever I hear the violins playing my sanity for a fool, I am almost certain that a string will brake as soon as my heart opens up...Mistake me for a coward - I can't care any less. It's the symphony that counts all together!

ME, MYSELF, AND IVANA

I SURRENDER

Share your fragile inequity
for the sake of revelation and consent,
as I stay lightly amused
faking a heartbeat faster than sunbeam
witnessing my shadow of existence.

> Dare to venture my point of view
> of a universal ground of benevolence
> where all right is wrong
> and the left-handed are taking over the world...

> Is evaporation retrieval?

Numb and steady I hear your voice
in the long run leading me back to myself
'cause I smell the fear of your words
infatuated by the weep of your soul
whenever I look up,
and I only look up to remember
that the light is visible
if one has courtesy for discrimination.

> Steps and sighs
> mark my future of oblivion
> and I smile only where you can't feel me.

> And you feel me forever...

Slow fade closing a final chapter: I sit with my eyes closed, my ears covered, and I only see and hear of you! Numb the distance between time and time again when I was a mildly different version of myself from what I am today...Rocking forward and backward...Forever and ever crunched like a nutshell cracked but never opened. What a sight for your sore eyes! If only you could smell my aching soul from miles away...You'd smile for the sake of all that is left unsaid and I know you only wanted to say: Leave now before I break you!

IVANA KOROVESOVSKA

FAMOUS LAST WORDS

While I shiver with a pleasant delight
of a memory colored in dark white
I secretly wish for an impious to hear
about a dreamland of my disappear.

Still as the night and cold as the day
merely breathing you from faraway
I awake from my everlasting sleep
pulling my grief down from the deep.

Steal me a passion with your gentle sound
and I'll convert my anger to the unfound
as I slowly close my window of hope
attached to my nightmare to a single rope.

I lost my reality before it came to life
and even though you are somebody else's wife
I feel your presence by the second
and wonder if you ever stop to reckon:
Can you really expect a newborn
made out from the heart you savagely torn?

The dead has spoken!

Numb is the dark angel living in the light of the night, fading with each falling star...Oh how I cried for the stars dying along the sidewalk, while the moon only shines for the one resting up above...The river of regret forms a revelation seen by the barely alive, and I hope they somehow drown their last fears and despair in the mud...Endurance is a bliss, and I pay the penalty for purity each time my heart remembers the empathy for the sky! FOREVER run smoothly...

AUTHOR BIO

Ivana Korovesovska was born May the 5th 1984, in Skopje Macedonia. Her native language is Macedonian. She studied high-school, and majored Interior design. She had and still has affinity toward arts (music, drawing...), she loves the English language as her own, and although in high-school she didn't like poetry that much, she somehow found a filter in its very essence ☺ She's a freelance designer at 99designs, and teaches Kung Fu in her spare time.

www.ingramcontent.com/pod-product-compliance
Lightning Source LLC
Chambersburg PA
CBHW020703300426
44112CB00007B/494